# Mother Manning Spiritual Cookbook

## by

## Mother Manning

auth‌orHOUSE™

*1663 Liberty Drive, Suite 200*
*Bloomington, Indiana 47403*
*(800) 839-8640*
*www.AuthorHouse.com*

© 2006 Mother Manning. All rights reserved.

No part of this book may be reproduced, stored in a retrieval system, or transmitted by any means without the written permission of the author.

First published by AuthorHouse 5/23/2006

ISBN: 1-4208-4361-3 (E)

ISBN: 1-4208-4360-5 (SC)

Printed in the United States of America
Bloomington, Indiana

This book is printed on acid-free paper.

# TABLE OF CONTENTS

## *Soups* ............................................................. *1*
    Fish Chowder ................................................. 3
    Fish Soup ...................................................... 4
    Fresh Tomato Soup ......................................... 5
    Onion Soup .................................................... 6
    Ox Tail Soup .................................................. 7
    Oyster soup .................................................... 8
    Shrimp and Cabbage Soup .............................. 9
    Shrimp and Chicken Soup ............................. 10

## *Salads* ........................................................... *11*
    Cabbage and Lettuce Salad ............................ 13
    Chicken Salad .............................................. 14
    Sweet Potato Salad ....................................... 15

## *Breads* .......................................................... *17*
    Bread and Biscuit Ideals ............................... 19
    Sausage Corn Bread ..................................... 20
    Brown Butter or Margarine ........................... 21
    Peanut Butter Mixture .................................. 22

## *Main Courses* ............................................... *23*
    Baked Chicken & Pineapples ......................... 25
    Bar-B-que Sauce ........................................... 26
    Bar-B-Que Steaks ......................................... 27
    Beef Pie ........................................................ 28
    Beef Roast .................................................... 29
    Beef Stew Casserole ..................................... 30
    Blackeye Peas .............................................. 31
    Cabbage and Sausage .................................... 32
    Cabbage with cheese ..................................... 33
    Cabbage with meal dumplings ....................... 34
    Cabbage-Ground Beef -Carrots ..................... 35
    Cat Fish Dish ............................................... 36
    Cheese and Bologna Toast ............................. 37
    Chicken and Cabbage ................................... 38
    Chicken and Cornmeal Dumplings ................ 39

| | |
|---|---|
| Chicken and Noodles | 40 |
| Chicken and Rice | 41 |
| Chicken Casserole | 42 |
| Chicken Dish | 43 |
| Chicken in Sour Cream | 44 |
| Chicken Liver Dish | 45 |
| Chicken or Turkey Baked in a Bag | 46 |
| Chop suey | 47 |
| Chopped Liver Dish | 48 |
| Collard Green Dish | 49 |
| Dish of Chicken | 50 |
| Egg Cups | 51 |
| Egg Dish | 52 |
| Egg Mixture | 53 |
| Floating Beef Roast | 54 |
| Fried Cabbage and Bacon | 55 |
| Glazed Chicken Dish | 56 |
| Green Beans and Potatoes | 57 |
| Grits and Ham | 58 |
| Ham Slices | 59 |
| Hot dog sour kraut | 60 |
| Hot Pepper Sauce | 61 |
| Lamb Chops | 62 |
| Lima Beans and Tomatoes | 63 |
| Lima Beans Dish | 64 |
| Lima Beans | 65 |
| Link Sausage Dish | 66 |
| Macaroni and Cheese Dish | 67 |
| Meat Loaf | 68 |
| Mix Beans | 69 |
| Mustard Greens | 70 |
| Onion Pie | 71 |
| Oven ribs | 72 |
| Pickled Pig Feet | 73 |
| Pork Chop Sandwich | 74 |
| Pot Beef Roast | 75 |
| Rabbit or Chicken Dumplings | 76 |

Red Rice ................................................................................... 77
Rice & Shrimp Dish ................................................................ 78
Scalloped Potatoes .................................................................. 79
Shalots onion dish .................................................................. 80
Sliced Liver ............................................................................. 81
Smothered Chicken ................................................................. 82
Sour Cream Chicken ............................................................... 83
Special Boiled Corn ................................................................ 84
Special Hot Dogs .................................................................... 85
Steak & Mushroom ................................................................. 86
Stew Meat ............................................................................... 87
Stuffed Cabbage ...................................................................... 88
Sunny Side Up Eggs ............................................................... 89
Sweet and Sour Dish ............................................................... 90
Sweet Pea Dumpling ............................................................... 91
Sweet Potatoe Balls ................................................................ 92
Sweet Potatoe Souffle ............................................................. 93
Traditional Beef Stew ............................................................. 94
Turkey Legs ............................................................................ 95
Veal Cutlets ............................................................................. 96

## *Desserts* ................................................................................ *97*
Cherry Cake ............................................................................ 99
Coconut Cookies ..................................................................... 100
Cookie Ideal ............................................................................ 101
Corn Bread Cake ..................................................................... 102
Corn Bread Pudding ................................................................ 103
Dream Cake ............................................................................ 104
Egg Custard Pie ...................................................................... 105
Egg Pudding ........................................................................... 106
Fruit Cake ............................................................................... 107
Green Tomato Pie ................................................................... 108
Hot Cocoa ............................................................................... 109
Ice Cream Cups ...................................................................... 110
Loaf Cake ............................................................................... 111
Oatmeal Cake ......................................................................... 112
Peach and Cabbage Cobbler ................................................... 113
Peach Cobbler ........................................................................ 114

| | |
|---|---|
| Peach Delight | 115 |
| Peach in a Blanket | 116 |
| Peach Parfait | 117 |
| Peach Pie | 118 |
| Peach Pudding | 119 |
| Poor Man's Pudding | 120 |
| Pound Cake | 121 |
| Rainbow Cake | 122 |
| Rainbow Pop Corn | 123 |
| Raisin Chiffon Pie | 124 |
| Raisin Delight Cake | 125 |
| Raisin Delight | 126 |
| Raspberry Pie | 127 |
| Rice Parfait | 128 |
| Rice Pudding | 129 |

# *Soups*

# Fish Chowder

| Amount | Measure | Ingredient -- Preparation Method |
|--------|---------|----------------------------------|
| 3 | cups | milk |
| 2 | tablespoons | corn starch |
| 1 | pound | halibut or cod diced |
| 1/2 | teaspoon | salt |
| 1/2 | teaspoon | pepper |
| 3 | tablespoons | butter |
| 1 | small | onion |
| 1/2 | cup | green peas |
| 1 | teaspoon | curry powder |
| 1 | teaspoon | sugar |
| 1 | rib | celery |

Combine all ingredients in pot. Add more milk if necessary and cook 20-30 minutes or until done.

*Mother Manning*

# Fish Soup

| Amount | Measure | Ingredient -- Preparation Method |
| --- | --- | --- |
| 1 1/2 | cups | cat or cod fish |
| 2 | cups | water |
| 1 1/2 | cups | milk |
| 1 | stick | butter |
| 1/2 | cup | celery cut up |
| 1 | medium | onion cut up |
|  | dash | salt and pepper |

Combine all ingredients and place in a large pot. Bring to a boil and then let simmer for 35-40 minutes. Serve hot with crackers.

# Fresh Tomato Soup

| Amount | Measure | Ingredient -- Preparation Method |
|--------|---------|----------------------------------|
| 4 | large | tomatoes cut up |
| 1/2 | cup | uncooked rice |
| 1/2 | cup | diced bologna |
| 1/2 | cup | celery cut up |
| 1/2 | cup | green pepper cut up |
| 1/2 | cup | corn |
| 1 | medium | onion cut up |
| 3 | cups | water |
| 1/2 | teaspoon | curry powder |
|  | dash | salt and pepper |

Combine tomatoes, uncooked rice, diced bologna, celery, green pepper, corn, and onions in a large pot. Cover with water and season with curry powder, salt and pepper. Cook about 30-40 minutes.

# Onion Soup

| Amount | Measure | Ingredient -- Preparation Method |
|---|---|---|
| 1 | pound | onion sliced |
| 2 | cups | water |
| 2 | cloves | garlic minced |
| 1 |  | potatoe cut up |
| 1/2 | cup | celery cut up |
| 1/2 | cup | carrots cut up |
| 1 | teaspoon | oregano |
| 1 | can | chicken broth |
|  |  | salt and pepper to taste |

Mix all ingredients in a large pot and cook for 30 to 35 minutes, or until done. This recipe is good for your health so enjoy.

# Ox Tail Soup

| Amount | Measure | Ingredient -- Preparation Method |
|---|---|---|
| 3 | pounds | ox tails |
| 1 | medium | onion |
| 1/2 | cup | celery cut up |
| 1/2 | cup | green pepper cut up |
| 1 | cup | mixed vegetables |
| 1 | large can | tomatoes |
| 1 | large | potato cut up |
| 2 | cloves | garlic |

Cover ox tails with water, season with salt and pepper to taste. Add remaining ingredients and cook until ox tails are tender.

# Oyster soup

| Amount | Measure | Ingredient -- Preparation Method |
| --- | --- | --- |
| 2 | cups | water |
| 2 | cups | milk |
| 1 | medium | onion cut up |
| 1 | small | potato thinly sliced |
| 1 | tablespoon | butter |
| 1 | can | oysters |
|  |  | salt and pepper to taste |

Mix all ingredients together, cook about 30 minutes. Serve with oyster crackers and enjoy.

# Shrimp and Cabbage Soup

| Amount | Measure | Ingredient -- Preparation Method |
|---|---|---|
| 1 |  | head of cabbage |
| 1/2 | pound | shrimp |
| 2 | cups | mixed vegetables |
| 1/2 | cup | uncooked rice |
| 2 | cups | lima bean |
| 1/2 | cup | celery |
| 1/2 | cup | green peppers |
| 1 | cup | onions cut up |
| 1 | can | tomatoes |
| 2 | cloves | garlic cut up |
| 2 | cups | okra cut up |
| 3 1/2 | quarts | water |
|  | dash | salt, pepper, hot pepper, sugar |

Add all ingredients to the 3 1/2 quarts of water. Season to taste with salt, pepper, sugar and hot pepper. Bring to a boil, then simmer for 1 hour and enjoy.

*Mother Manning*

# Shrimp and Chicken Soup

| Amount | Measure   | Ingredient -- Preparation Method   |
|--------|-----------|------------------------------------|
| 2      | cups      | chicken nuggets unbreaded          |
| 2      | cups      | shrimp                             |
| 1      | cup       | mixed vegetables                   |
| 1/2    | cup       | uncooked rice                      |
| 1      | cup       | lima bean                          |
| 1/2    | cup       | celery and green pepper            |
| 1      | cup       | onion cut up                       |
| 1      | large can | tomatoes                           |
| 2      | cloves    | garlic cut up                      |
| 2      | cups      | okra cut up                        |
| 3 1/2  | quarts    | water                              |
|        | dash      | salt, pepper, hot pepper and sugar |

Add all ingredients to the 3 1/2 quarts of water. Season to taste with salt, pepper, sugar and hot pepper. Bring to a boil, and then simmer for 1 hour. Enjoy

# *Salads*

# Cabbage and Lettuce Salad

| Amount | Measure | Ingredient -- Preparation Method |
| --- | --- | --- |
| 2 | cups | lettuce cut up |
| 1 1/2 | cups | cabbage (center cut up) |
| 1 | small | onion cut |
| 1/2 | cup | green pepper |
| 1/2 | cup | celery juice |
| 1/2 | cup | carrot |
| 1/2 | cup | apple |
|  | dash | salt, pepper, and sugar |
|  |  | your favorite dressing |

Chop up all ingredients and toss together. Season with salt, pepper and sugar. Serve with your favorite dressing.

# Chicken Salad

| Amount | Measure | Ingredient -- Preparation Method |
| --- | --- | --- |
| 2 | cups | diced cooked chicken |
| 1/2 | | head of shredded lettuce |
| 1 | small | apple chopped |
| 1 | medium | onion chopped up |
| 1/2 | cup | green pepper |
| 1/2 | cup | celery |
| 1/2 | cup | cooked green peas |
| | dash | sugar |
| 1 | small | tomato cut up |
| | | your favorite dressing |

Toss lettuce, diced chicken, apple pieces, onion, green pepper, celery, green peas, and sugar. Add tomatoes and sprinkle with salt and pepper to taste. Serve with your favorite dressing and enjoy.

# Sweet Potato Salad

| Amount | Measure | Ingredient -- Preparation Method |
|--------|---------|----------------------------------|
| 1 | cup | sweet potatoes cooked |
| 1 | cup | marshmallow |
| 1 | cup | apples |
|   |   | sugar to taste |
|   |   | slaw dressing |

Dice and mix sweet potatoes, marshmallows, and apples. Add a little sugar to taste. Dress with slaw dressing, Serve with meats and vegetables.

# *Breads*

# Bread and Biscuit Ideals

| Amount | Measure | Ingredient -- Preparation Method |
|--------|---------|----------------------------------|
|        |         | breads                           |

When making bread add cheese to the dough. Fry a small patty in a frying pan with oil. Brown on both sides. Serve hot with syrup.

# Sausage Corn Bread

| Amount | Measure | Ingredient -- Preparation Method |
| --- | --- | --- |
| 1/2 | pound | link sausage |
|  |  | corn bread mixture |

Arrange sausage pieces on bottom of baking pan. Make your corn bread or use prepacked corn bread. Pour corn bread mixture over sausage. Bake until brown and done.

Alternative: pour into muffin pan and just before baking sprinkle crumbled bacon mixed with corn meal or top. Grated cheese can also be used as a topping. Bake for 25-30 minutes in a 350 degree oven.

# Brown Butter or Margarine

| Amount | Measure | Ingredient -- Preparation Method |
|---|---|---|
| 3 | sticks | butter or margarine very soft |
| 1 | tablespoon | cocoa powder |

Take very soft butter or margarine and add cocoa to it. Mix Well until very brown. Great on toast.

# Peanut Butter Mixture

| Amount | Measure | Ingredient -- Preparation Method |
| --- | --- | --- |
| 1 1/2 | cups | peanut butter |
| 1/2 | cup | honey |
| 3-4 | | strips of bacon |

Cook and crumble bacon until fine. Mix peanut butter, honey and bacon together. Spread on bread. Enjoy!

# *Main Courses*

# Baked Chicken & Pineapples

| Amount | Measure | Ingredient -- Preparation Method |
| --- | --- | --- |
| 1 | | chicken split in half |
| 1 | cup | pineapple juice |
| | | salt and pepper |
| 1 | cup | reserve pineapple juice for sauce |
| 1 1/2 | tablespoons | corn starch |
| 3 | tablespoons | butter |
| | dash | nutmeg |
| 1 1/2 | tablespoons | brown sugar |
| 1 | cup | water |
| | | pineapple slices |
| | | tooth picks |

Season chicken with salt and pepper on both sides, place into a baking dish with 1 cup of pineapple juice. Bake for 30 minutes in a 300 degree oven. Make sauce by combining pineapple juice, corn starch, butter, nutmeg, brown sugar, and water, cook until thick. Spread sauce on the chicken then using the tooth picks place a few pineapple slices on the chicken and bake for another 20-25 minutes.

*Mother Manning*

# Bar-B-que Sauce

| Amount | Measure | Ingredient -- Preparation Method |
| --- | --- | --- |
| 2 | cups | tomato sauce |
| 2 | cups | tomato ketchup |
| 1/2 | cup | brown sugar |
| 1/2 | | lemon sliced |
| | dash | hot sauce |
| 1 | small | onion slice |
| 1/2 | stick | butter |
| 1 1/2 | tablespoons | vinegar |
| 1 | teaspoon | vanilla flavoring |
| | dash | nutmeg |

Mix all ingredients together and let simmer for 25-30 minutes until thicken. Adjust to your taste, serve with any BBQ meats.

# Bar-B-Que Steaks

| Amount | Measure | Ingredient -- Preparation Method |
| --- | --- | --- |
|   |   | steak |
| 2 | tablespoons | lemon juice or vinegar |
| 1 | cup | water |
|   |   | barbecue sauce |

Season steaks with salt and pepper on both sides. Place on grill, and as you turn steaks baste each side with lemon juice and water. When just about done baste each side with barbecue sauce.

# Beef Pie

| Amount | Measure | Ingredient -- Preparation Method |
| --- | --- | --- |
| 2 1/2 | cups | cooked beef |
| 1 1/2 | cups | sugar |
| 2 | tablespoons | cornstarch |
| 1 | teaspoon | vanilla extract |
|  | dash | nutmeg |
| 1 | stick | butter |
| 2 | tablespoons | vinegar |
| 1 |  | pie crust |

Mix all ingredients together, cook 3-4 minutes. Place ingredients in pie shell, cover with addition crust and make 3 to 4 slits in crust top. Bake 45 minutes in a 300 degree oven or until done.

# Beef Roast

| Amount | Measure | Ingredient -- Preparation Method |
| --- | --- | --- |
| 1 | medium | beef roast |
| 1 | teaspoon | tarragon or sage |
| 1 | teaspoon | salt |
| 1/2 | teaspoon | black pepper |
| 3 | tablespoons | flour |
| 1 | medium | onion |
|  | sliced | green peppers |
|  |  | celery slices |
| 1 | cup | beef broth or water |

Mix tarragon, salt, pepper, and flour. Next rub all over the roast. Place in roasting pan, surround with onion, green pepper, and celery slices. Add 1 cup of beef broth or water and bake for 1 hour in a 350 degree oven or until done.

*Mother Manning*

# Beef Stew Casserole

| Amount | Measure | Ingredient -- Preparation Method |
| --- | --- | --- |
| 2 | cups | cooked rice |
| 1/2 | cup | chicken broth |
| 1 | can | beef stew |
|  |  | sliced cheese |

Spread 2 cups of cooked rice on bottom of baking dish. Add 1/2 cup of chicken broth. Top with 1 can of beef stew and slices of cheese. Bake until cheese is melted in a 275 degree oven.

# Blackeye Peas

| Amount | Measure | Ingredient -- Preparation Method |
|---|---|---|
| 1 | pound | blackeyed peas |
|  | pinch | soda |
| 1 | pound | jowel bacon or ham diced |
| 1 | teaspoon | salt |
| 1 | teaspoon | sugar or honey |
| 1 | tablespoon | chili powder |
| 1 | teaspoon | tarragon |
| 3 | tablespoons | oil |
| 1 | medium | onion cut up |

Clean and wash blackeyed peas. Place in a pot of hot boiling water and let sit for 30 minutes. Drain water and fill pot again with hot water. Add jowel or ham, soda, salt, sugar, chili powder, tarragon, oil and diced onions. Cook for 40 minutes or until done.

# Cabbage and Sausage

| Amount | Measure | Ingredient -- Preparation Method |
| --- | --- | --- |
| 1 | small | cabbage cut up |
| 1 | medium | onion diced |
| 1/2 | cup | green pepper diced |
| 2 | ribs | celery diced |
| 1 | pound | smoke sausage cut up |
| 2 | teaspoons | sugar |
|  | dash | salt and pepper |
| 1/2 | cup | carrots diced |
| 1 1/2 | cups | water |
| 4 | tablespoons | oil or butter |

Combine all ingredients in a large pot with water and oil. Cook for 25 minutes or until cabbage is tender. Then serve.

# Cabbage with cheese

| Amount | Measure | Ingredient -- Preparation Method |
| --- | --- | --- |
| 1 | small | cabbage |
| 1 1/2 | cups | water |
| 1 | teaspoon | salt |
| 1 | teaspon | sugar |
|  | dash | pepper |
| 3 | tablespoons | oil or butter |

Place cabbage in pot with water then season with salt, sugar, pepper and oil. Cook for 25 minutes. Place a few slices of cheese on top and cook for an additional 15 minutes.

*Mother Manning*

# Cabbage with meal dumplings

| Amount | Measure | Ingredient -- Preparation Method |
| --- | --- | --- |
| 1 |  | cabbage head |
|  |  | meat balls |
|  |  | meal dumplings |
|  |  | salt and pepper |
|  | dash | sugar |
| 1/2 | cup | green pepper |
| 1 | small can | vegetable soup |
| 3 | tablespoons | butter or oil |
| 2 1/2 | cups | water |
|  |  | tooth picks |

Take and put aside a few loose leaves of the cabbage. Make a hallow into the cabbage, and fill with small meat balls and meal dumplings. Season with salt, pepper and a dash of sugar. Add onion, green peppers, vegetable soup, and butter or oil. Pour in the water, and cover with cabbage leaves. Pin down the leaves with tooth picks, and cook for 30 to 35 minutes in 350 degree oven.

# Cabbage-Ground Beef -Carrots

| Amount | Measure | Ingredient -- Preparation Method |
| --- | --- | --- |
| 1 | | cabbage head |
| 1/2 | cup | onion |
| 1/2 | cup | green peppers |
| | dash | salt |
| | dash | pepper |
| | dash | sugar |
| 1/2 | cup | carrot |
| 1/2 | cup | tomatoes |
| 2 1/2 | cups | water |
| 2 | tablespoons | oil |
| | | ground beef patties |

Pour oil into bottom of baking dish. Next make a layer of cabbage. On top of the layer of cabbage put onions and green pepper. Next sprinkle with salt, pepper, and sugar. Make a large seasoned hamburger pattie, place on top of cabbage mixture. Then repeat the layer as above, but top with sliced carrots and sliced tomatoes. add water and bake covered in a 350 degree oven until done. Cabbage is
done when tender.

# Cat Fish Dish

| Amount | Measure | Ingredient -- Preparation Method |
| --- | --- | --- |
| 2 1/2 | pounds | cat fish nuggets |
| 1 |  | egg |
| 1 | cup | flour |
|  | dash | salt and pepper |
|  |  | water |

First make batter with egg, flour, salt and pepper. Add enough water to make a paste. Then season catfish nuggets to your taste. Next dip nuggets into batter and deep fry in hot oil until brown. Enjoy!

# Cheese and Bologna Toast

| Amount | Measure | Ingredient -- Preparation Method |
|--------|---------|----------------------------------|
| 1 | slice | bread buttered on both sides |
| 1 |  | bologna slice |
| 1 | slice | cheese |

Place bologna on bread and toast under broiler until cheese is melted. Serve hot. Crisp bacon may be substituted for bologna.

*Mother Manning*

# Chicken and Cabbage

| Amount | Measure | Ingredient -- Preparation Method |
|---|---|---|
| 1 | whole | chicken |
| 1 | small | cabbage |
| 1/2 | cup | carrot |
| 1/2 | cup | onion |
|  |  | oil |
|  | dash | salt and pepper |
|  | dash | paprika |
|  | dash | sugar |

Season chicken with salt, pepper, and paprika. Rub spices all over the chicken inside and out. Put layer of cabbage, sliced onion and carrots on the bottom of pan. Put 1/2 cup of cabbage inside the chicken. Season the cabbage with a little sugar, salt and pepper. Then place chicken on top of cabbage with 1 1/2 cup of water and a little of oil. Bake in a 350 degree oven until done.

# Chicken and Cornmeal Dumplings

| Amount | Measure | Ingredient -- Preparation Method |
|--------|---------|----------------------------------|
| 1 | medium | onion chopped up |
| 1/2 | cup | green pepper chopped up |
|  |  | chicken parts |
|  |  | corn bread mixture |

Season chicken with salt and pepper to taste. Next boil chicken with chopped up onions and green pepper. Boil until chicken is done. Take corn bread mixture (not to soft) and drop spoonful into chicken. Then cook about 15 more minutes and serve hot.

*Mother Manning*

# Chicken and Noodles

| Amount | Measure | Ingredient -- Preparation Method |
|---|---|---|
| | | chicken parts |
| | | chicken broths |
| 2 | cups | flour |
| 1 1/2 | tablespoons | molasses |
| 3 1/2 | tablespoons | oil |
| | | water |

Boil chicken until almost done with water and chicken broth. Season to taste with salt, pepper and 1/2 stick of butter. Make noodles with flour, molasses, and oil, adding just enough water to form a stiff ball of dough. Roll out dough and cut into strips. Drop stripes into boiling chicken and broth and cook 20 minutes. Make sure chicken is completely done and serve hot.

# Chicken and Rice

| Amount | Measure | Ingredient -- Preparation Method |
|--------|---------|----------------------------------|
| 2 | cups | cooked chicken |
| 1 1/2 | cups | cooked rice |
| 1 | small | onion chopped |
| 1/2 | cup | green pepper |
| 2 | ribs | celery cut up |
| 1 | can | tomatoes |
| 1 | can | cream of chicken soup |
| 2 | cups | water |
| 1 | stick | butter |
| 2 | teaspoons | tarragon |
|  | dash | salt and pepper |

Combine all ingredients together in a large pot or skillet and cook for 25 minutes.

*Mother Manning*

# Chicken Casserole

| Amount | Measure | Ingredient -- Preparation Method |
| --- | --- | --- |
| 1 | whole | chicken cut up |
| 1 1/2 | cups | uncooked rice |
| 1 | can | tomatoes |
| 2 | cans | chicken broth |
| 2 | cups | water |
| 1/3 | cup | green pepper |
| 1/3 | cup | celery |
| 1 | medium | onion cut up |
| 1 1/2 | sticks | butter |
| 1 1/2 | tablespoons | tarragon |

Preheat oven to 375. Season chicken to taste. Boil chicken in pot for 15 minutes. Remove chicken from pot and place in large baking dish. Add remaining ingredients (except tarragon) and pour over chicken. Sprinkle tarragon on top and bake for 35-40 minutes or until done.

# Chicken Dish

| Amount | Measure | Ingredient -- Preparation Method |
| --- | --- | --- |
| 1 | whole | chicken cut into parts |
|  | dash | salt and pepper |
|  |  | flour |
| 1 | cup | oil |
| 1 | medium | onion |
| 1/2 | cup | green pepper |
| 1 | can | cream of chicken soup |
| 1 1/2 | tablespoons | flour or cornstarch |
| 2 | cups | water |

Heat 1 cup of oil in a frying pan. Coat cut up chicken parts with flour, salt, and pepper. Brown the chicken on both sides in the hot oil. Pour most of the oil off once chicken is brown. Next add cut up onion and green pepper. Then stir in cream of chicken soup, flour (cornstarch) and water. Mix all together and cook for 25-30 minutes.

*Mother Manning*

# Chicken in Sour Cream

| Amount | Measure | Ingredient -- Preparation Method |
|--------|---------|----------------------------------|
|        |         | chicken parts                    |
|        |         | flour                            |
|        |         | sour cream                       |

Season chicken, then coat with flour. Next roll in sour cream and bake at 375 degree until done.

# Chicken Liver Dish

| Amount | Measure | Ingredient -- Preparation Method |
|--------|---------|----------------------------------|
| 1 | pound | chicken liver |
| 1/2 | cup | flour |
|  |  | salt and pepper to taste |
| 4 | tablespoons | oil |
| 1 | small | onion sliced |
|  |  | Thick Batter |
| 1 1/2 | cups | flour |
| 1 | teaspoon | baking powder |
| 1 |  | egg |
| 3 | tablespoons | water |
| 4 | tablespoons | oil |
|  | dash | salt |

Season chicken livers with salt and pepper. Then coat in flour and fry in oil until done. Place in a baking dish with sliced onions. Cover this with the thick batter and bake until brown, about 20 minutes in a 350 degree oven.

*Mother Manning*

# Chicken or Turkey Baked in a Bag

| Amount | Measure | Ingredient -- Preparation Method |
|---|---|---|
| 1 | whole | chicken or turkey |
|   |   | salt and pepper |
|   |   | poultry seasoning |
|   |   | garlic powder |
|   |   | cooking oil |
|   |   | few strips of green pepper, celery and onion |
| 4 | cups | water |
| 4 | sticks | carrots |
|   |   | brown sugar |
|   |   | butter |

Slice green pepper, celery, onions, and carrots, place to the side. Rub meat well with cooking oil, then season with salt, pepper, poultry seasoning and garlic powder. Place bird in cooking bag with strips of celery, green pepper, and onion. Bake as directed on cooking bag package. On the outside of the bag, but in the same pan add carrot sticks and water. Bake 25-30 in a 350 degree oven. When carrots are done place in bowl and season with brown sugar and butter. This makes a nice side dish.

# Chop suey

| Amount | Measure | Ingredient -- Preparation Method |
| --- | --- | --- |
| 1 | cup | chopped dried beef |
| 1/2 | cup | chopped onion |
| 1/2 | cup | green pepper |
| 1/2 | cup | celery |
| 1 | can | chop seuy vegetables |
| 1/2 | can | bean sprouts |
| 2 | tablespoons | cornstarch |
| 1 1/2 | cups | water |
| 1 | tablespoon | pepper |
| 1 | tablespoon | salt |
|  | dash | sugar |

Mix all ingredents together, then cook for 25 to 30 minutes. Serve on rice or chowmein noodles.

*Mother Manning*

# Chopped Liver Dish

| Amount | Measure | Ingredient -- Preparation Method |
| --- | --- | --- |
| 1 | pound | liver chopped |
| 1 | medium | onion |
| 1/2 | cup | green pepper cut up |
| 1 | cup | flour |
| 1 | | egg |
| 1 | teaspoon | baking powder |
| 2 | tablespoons | oil |
| 1/2 | cup | milk |

Dip liver in mixture of milk, egg, salt, pepper, and baking powder. Then coat liver with flour, onion, and green pepper. Fry in hot oil until done.

# Collard Green Dish

| Amount | Measure | Ingredient -- Preparation Method |
| --- | --- | --- |
| 3 | pounds | collard greens cut up with meat of choice |
| 4 | cups | water |
| 1 | cup | milk |
| 1 | | green pepper cut up |
| 3 | tablespoons | oil |
| 3 | tablespoons | salt |
| 2 | teaspoons | sugar |
| | pinch | baking soda |

Cook meat in water for 15 minutes. Add collards, milk and green pepper. Season with salt, sugar, baking soda and oil. Cook 45-50 minutes.

*Mother Manning*

# Dish of Chicken

| Amount | Measure | Ingredient -- Preparation Method |
|---|---|---|
| 1 | whole | chicken |
| 1 | cup | oil |
| 1 | medium | onion |
| 1/2 | cup | green pepper |
| 1 | can | cream of chicken soup |
| 1 1/2 | tablespoons | flour or cornstarch |
| 2 | cups | water |

Heat oil in frying pan. Season chicken to taste and coat with flour. Brown chicken on both sides. Pour off most of the cooking oil and add onions and green peppers. Stir in cream of chicken soup flour or cornstarch and water. Stir and cook for 25-30 minutes or until done.

# Egg Cups

| Amount | Measure | Ingredient -- Preparation Method |
| --- | --- | --- |
| 6 |  | eggs |
| 4 | slices | bacon, fried to a crisp |
| 1 | small | chopped onion |
| 1/4 | cup | shredded American cheese |
|  |  | salad dressing |

Fry bacon until crisp. Boil eggs until firm. Cut eggs in half, remove yolk, mix yolk with crumbled bacon, chopped onions, cheese and salad dressing. Mix well, fill egg cups with mixture.

*Mother Manning*

# Egg Dish

| Amount | Measure | Ingredient -- Preparation Method |
|---|---|---|
| 1/2 | cup | shredded cheese |
| 1/2 | cup | onion |
| 1/2 | cup | green pepper |
| 1/2 | cup | bamboo shoots |
| 3 | tablespoons | oil |
| 4 | | beaten eggs |
| | salt and pepper to taste | |

Saute onions, green pepper, and bamboo shoots for 3 minutes in 3 tbsp of oil. Then add 4 eggs beaten, and cheese. Season to taste with salt and pepper and cook until eggs are done. Serve hot and enjoy.

# Egg Mixture

| Amount | Measure | Ingredient -- Preparation Method |
|--------|---------|----------------------------------|
| 4 | slices | cooked bacon or sausage |
| 1/2 | cup | onion cut up |
| 1/2 | cup | green pepper cut up |
| 1/2 | cup | lettuce cut up |
| 4 | eggs | beaten |

Add onions, green peppers, lettuce, and cooked meat to heated skillet. Add eggs and cook until done.

*Mother Manning*

# Floating Beef Roast

| Amount | Measure | Ingredient -- Preparation Method |
| --- | --- | --- |
| 3 | pounds | beef roast |
| 1 | medium | onion |
| 1/2 | cup | green pepper |
| 1/2 | cup | celery |
| 1/2 | cup | carrot |
| 1 | can | vegetable beef soup |
| 2 1/2 | cups | water |
| 7 | tablespoons | flour or cornstarch |
|  | dash | salt and pepper |
|  | dash | sage |

Season beef roast with salt, pepper and sage, then roll in 3-4 tbsp of flour. Brown on both sides in 4-5 tbsp of oil. Place into a pot, then add onion, green pepper, celery, and carrots. Next add vegetable beef soup and water. Slow cook about 40-45 minutes. Make a paste with 2 tbsp of flour or cornstarch. Add to roast along with more water if needed. Cook an additional 25-30 minutes and enjoy.

# Fried Cabbage and Bacon

| Amount | Measure | Ingredient -- Preparation Method |
|--------|---------|----------------------------------|
| 1 | small | cabbage |
| 1 | small | onion |
| 3 | strips | bacon fried crisp |
| 1 | cup | water |
|   | dash | sugar |
|   | dash | salt and pepper |

Cut up cabbage and onion. Fry bacon and set aside.
Add 2 tablespoons oil. Put cabbage and onions into frying pan with one cup of water. Season with salt and pepper and a dash of sugar. Finally stir fry about 15 minutes or until done. Serve hot.

*Mother Manning*

# Glazed Chicken Dish

| Amount | Measure | Ingredient -- Preparation Method |
| --- | --- | --- |
| 2 1/2 | cups | cooked chicken cut up |
| 1 1/2 | cups | pineapple bits |
| 1/2 | cup | diced onion |
| 1/2 | cup | diced celery |
| 1/2 | cup | diced green bell pepper |
| 1 | cup | zucchini cut up |
| 2 | teaspoons | flour or cornstarch |
| 2 | cups | water |
|  | dash | salt and pepper |

Mix chicken, pineapple bits, onion, celery, green pepper and zucchini. Heat 3 tbsp of oil in skillet and stir fry mixture for about 5 minutes. Make a paste with 2 tbsp flour or cornstarch. Add to mixture and stir well. Season with salt and pepper to taste. then add 2 cups of water. Finally cook for 15-20 minutes, and serve over rice.

# Green Beans and Potatoes

| Amount | Measure | Ingredient -- Preparation Method |
|--------|-------------|----------------------------------|
| 3 | cups | green beans cut up |
| 1 | small | onion cut up |
| 3 | potatoes | cut up |
| 1 | teaspoon | vinegar |
| 1 | teaspoon | sugar |
| 1 | teaspoon | salt and pepper |
| 3 | tablespoons | oil or butter |

Place all ingredients in pot and cover with water. Bring to a boil, and then simmer for 40 minutes or until done.

*Mother Manning*

# Grits and Ham

| Amount | Measure | Ingredient -- Preparation Method |
|--------|---------|----------------------------------|
|        |         | grits                            |
| 1/2    | cup     | cooked ham                       |
|        |         | butter                           |

Prepare grits as instructed on box. Add ham and butter to grits when almost done.

# Ham Slices

| Amount | Measure | Ingredient -- Preparation Method |
|---|---|---|
| 4 | slices | ham |
| 1 1/2 | tablespoons | corn starch |
| 4 | tablespoons | water |
| 1 1/2 | cups | orange juice |
| 3 | tablespoons | raisins |
| 4 | tablespoons | brown sugar |
|  | dash | cinnamon |

Bake ham slices for 20 minutes. Add corn starch, water, orange juice, raisins, brown sugar and cinnamon to sauce pan. Cook until thicken, pour over ham slices and cook for another 15 minutes.

# Hot dog sour kraut

| Amount | Measure | Ingredient -- Preparation Method |
|---|---|---|
| 1 | can | sour kraut drained well |
| 1 | pound | hot dogs cut up into halves |
| 1 | cup | sliced apples |
| 3 | tablespoons | brown sugar |
|   |   | salt and pepper to taste |
| 3 | tablespoons | butter |

Mix sour kraut with hotdog, and season with salt and pepper. Cut up sliced apple, brown sugar and butter. Heat and serve hot.

# Hot Pepper Sauce

| Amount | Measure | Ingredient -- Preparation Method |
|--------|---------|----------------------------------|
| 2 | cloves | garlic |
| 4 |  | hot peppers |
| 1 | small | onion |
|  | dash | salt. pepper, sugar and vinegar |

Chop up garlic, peppers, and onions, place in jar. Add a dash of salt, pepper and sugar. Cover with vinegar and close.

# Lamb Chops

| Amount | Measure | Ingredient -- Preparation Method |
| --- | --- | --- |
| 1 1/2 | pounds | lamb chops |
| 1/2 | cup | water |
| 2 | tablespoons | lemon juice |
| | | salt and pepper to taste |
| | | **2nd variation** |
| 1 | small | onion chopped |
| | | tarragon & poultry season |
| | | salt and pepper |
| | | flour |

Season lamb chops with salt and pepper, then place into a baking dish. Add water, and sprinkle with lemon juice. Bake for 25-30 minutes in 375 degree oven or until done. turn once during baking.

2nd variation: Season lamb chops with salt, pepper and flour. Line bottom of baking pan with chopped onion. Place lamb chops in baking pan, sprinkle with tarragon and poultry season. Add 1/2 cup of water. Finally bake until done and enjoy.

# Lima Beans and Tomatoes

| Amount | Measure | Ingredient -- Preparation Method |
| --- | --- | --- |
| 2 | cups | fresh lima beans |
| 1 1/2 | cups | fresh tomatoes cut up |
| 1 | small | onion cut up |
| 1/2 | cup | green pepper cut up |
|  | dash | salt and pepper |
|  | dash | sugar |
| 1 | stick | butter |
| 2 1/2 | cups | water |

Combine all ingredient, then cook for 40 minutes or until done.

# Lima Beans Dish

| Amount | Measure | Ingredient -- Preparation Method |
|---|---|---|
| 1 | package | frozen lima beans |
| 1/2 | stick | butter |
| 1 | teaspoon | sugar |
| 1 | large | potato sliced |
| 1 | medium | onion slice |
|  | dash | salt and pepper |
|  |  | milk or water |
|  |  | cheese |

Place lima beans into a baking dish with sliced potato and onion slices. Season mixture with salt and pepper, then cover with milk or water. Bake 25-30 minutes in a 325 degree oven. When almost done spread with cheese slices on top and cook until cheese is melted. Serve hot and enjoy.

# Lima Beans

| Amount | Measure | Ingredient -- Preparation Method |
|--------|---------|----------------------------------|
| 2 | cups | cooked lima beans |
| 1 | small | onions |
| 1 | teaspoon | sugar |
| 1/2 | stick | butter |
|   | dash | salt and pepper |
|   |   | cheese |
|   |   | milk or water |

Place 2 cups of cooked lima beans into a baking dish with 1small onion cut up. Add 1 tsp sugar, 1/2 stick of butter. Then season with salt and pepper to taste. Cover with milk or water. Bake about 25 minutes in a 350 degree oven. when almost done top with cheese and cook until cheese is melted. Serve hot.

*Mother Manning*

# Link Sausage Dish

| Amount | Measure | Ingredient -- Preparation Method |
| --- | --- | --- |
|  |  | 4-5 link sausages |
|  |  | corn bread mixture or stove top stuffing |

Split apart link sausage, fill each with corn bread or stuffing. Bake for 30 minutes in a 350 degree oven or until done.

# Macaroni and Cheese Dish

| Amount | Measure | Ingredient -- Preparation Method |
|--------|---------|----------------------------------|
|        |         | macaroni and cheese              |
|        |         | bread crumbs                     |
|        |         | melted butter                    |
|        |         | red food coloring                |

Prepare your favorite macaroni and cheese dish or use a store mix. Make as usual. Mix bread crumbs with melted butter and a few drops of red food coloring. Stir lightly and spread on top of macaroni. Bake until brown in a 350 degree oven.

*Mother Manning*

# Meat Loaf

| Amount | Measure | Ingredient -- Preparation Method |
| --- | --- | --- |
| 1 1/2 | pounds | ground beef |
|  | dash | salt and pepper |
| 1/2 | cup | green pepper |
| 1/2 | cup | onions |
| 1 |  | egg |
| 2 | tablespoons | flour or oatmeal |
| 1 | small can | tomato sauce or ketchup |
| 1/2 | cup | shredded American cheese |
|  | dash | worcestershire sauce |

Combine ground beef. salt, pepper, green pepper, onions, egg and flour (oatmeal) with tomato sauce. Mix well and shape into a loaf. Make a opening in the middle of loaf and fill with cheese. Cover top of loaf with tomato ketchup and worcestershire sauce. Bake at 325 for 30 minutes.

# Mix Beans

| Amount | Measure | Ingredient -- Preparation Method |
| --- | --- | --- |
| 1/2 | cup | navy, pinto, kidney, and great northern beans |
| 1 | small | onion diced |
| 2 | tablespoons | molasses or honey |
|  | pinch | salt, pepper and soda |
|  | dash | chili powder |
| 4 | tablespoons | oil |
|  | piece | ham, salt pork, or jowl bacon |
|  |  | water |

Soak beans in a pan covered with hot water for 30 minutes., After 30 minutes change the water and cover with hot water again. Season with onion, molasses, salt, pepper, and chili powder. Add a pinch of soda and pieces of ham, salt pork or jowl bacon. Cook for about 1 hour or until done. Add more water as needed.

*Mother Manning*

# Mustard Greens

| Amount | Measure | Ingredient -- Preparation Method |
| --- | --- | --- |
| 3 | pounds | mustard greens |
|  |  | ham or salt pork to taste |
| 4 | teaspoons | oil |
|  | pinch | of baking soda |
| 5 | cups | water |

Boil meat in 5 cups of water for about 15 minutes. Add greens, season to taste with salt, sugar, pinch of soda and oil. Slow cook for 1 hour.

# Onion Pie

| Amount | Measure | Ingredient -- Preparation Method |
| --- | --- | --- |
| 2 | cups | sliced onion |
|  | dash | salt and pepper |
|  | dash | sugar |
| 2 | tablespoons | flour |
| 2 | tablespoons | oil or butter |
| 2 | tablespoons | water |
|  |  | pie crust |

Put onion slices in pie pan, and season with salt, pepper, and dash of sugar. Add flour, oil, and water. Pour over onions. Cover with crust and make 3-5 slits in crust. Bake 20-25 minutes in a 250 degree oven. Serve as side dish with meats.

# Oven ribs

| Amount | Measure | Ingredient -- Preparation Method |
|---|---|---|
| 1 | slab | pork ribs |
| | | salt and pepper to taste |
| 3 | cups | water or apple juice |
| 1 | can | sour kraut drained |
| 3 1/2 | tablespoons | brown sugar |
| 2 | | sliced apples |
| 2 | tablespoons | vinegar |
| 1 | | diced onion |

Season ribs with salt and pepper. Place in bottom of roaster. Next cover with water or apple juice, and cook for 40 minutes. Add sour kraut drained, brown sugar, vinegar, onion, and sliced apples. Cook until done. Add more Juice or water as needed. This recipe may also be used on pork chops or beef ribs.

# Pickled Pig Feet

| Amount | Measure | Ingredient -- Preparation Method |
|---|---|---|
| 4 |  | pig's feet |
| 1/2 | cup | vinegar |
|  | dash | groung hot pepper |
| 1 | small | onion |
| 1/2 | cup | green pepper cut up |
| 1/2 | cup | celery cut up |

Wash pig feet and put into pot. Season with salt and pepper to your taste, cover with water. Add vinegar, ground hot pepper , onion, green pepper and celery. Cook about 1 1/2 hours or until done. Add water as needed.

*Mother Manning*

# Pork Chop Sandwich

| Amount | Measure | Ingredient -- Preparation Method |
|--------|---------|----------------------------------|

When making a pork chop sandwich use honey instead of salad dressing. Spread honey on your bread.

# Pot Beef Roast

| Amount | Measure | Ingredient -- Preparation Method |
| --- | --- | --- |
| 2 1/2 | pounds | pot roast |
| 1/2 | cup | flour |
| 3 | tablespoons | oil |
| 1 1/2 | cups | water |
| 2 | cups | tomato sauce or juice |
| 1 | small | onion |
| 1/2 | cup | chopped green pepper & celery |
| 1 | teaspoon | tarragon |
| 1/2 | cup | carrots |
|  |  | salt and pepper to taste |

Season pot roast, and roll in flour. Heat oil in pan, then brown rolled pot roast on both sides. Place browned pot roast in pan with water, tomato sauce, onion, green pepper, celery, and carrots. Season with tarragon, salt and pepper. (potatoes can also be added if desired). Bake covered in a 350 degree oven for about 2 hours. More water may be added if needed.

*Mother Manning*

# Rabbit or Chicken Dumplings

| Amount | Measure | Ingredient -- Preparation Method |
|---|---|---|
| 1 | small | onion cut up |
| 1/4 | cup | celery cut up |
| 1 | tablespoon | salt |
| 1 | teaspoon | pepper and sage |
| 2 | tablespoons | butter |
| 1 | can | biscuits |

Season rabbit or chicken with salt, pepper, butter and sage. Place in pot, then add onion and celery. Cover with water and bring to a boil. Cook for about 45 minutes. Keep covered with water. Roll can of biscuits flat. Cut biscuits into small pieces or blocks add to rabbit or chicken mixture. Cook an additional 20 minutes or until tender. Serve hot.

# Red Rice

| Amount | Measure | Ingredient -- Preparation Method |
|--------|---------|----------------------------------|
|        |         | cooked rice                      |
|        |         | red food coloring                |

For a nice change, or to add color to a special recipe add a few drops of red food coloring when cooking rice.

*Mother Manning*

# Rice & Shrimp Dish

| Amount | Measure | Ingredient -- Preparation Method |
|---|---|---|
| 2 1/2 | cups | cooked rice |
| 2 | cups | shrimp |
| 1 1/2 | Cups | chicken broth |
|  | dash | curry powder |
|  | dash | salt and pepper |

Preheat oven to 350 degree. Spread the bottom of a baking dish with cooked rice. Cover the rice with shrimp. Season to taste with salt and pepper. Add the chicken broth and sprinkle with curry powder. Bake about 20 or 30 minutes. Serve hot.

# Scalloped Potatoes

| Amount | Measure | Ingredient -- Preparation Method |
|--------|---------|----------------------------------|
|        |         | Sliced potatoes |
|        |         | Sliced onions |
|        |         | cheese sliced |
|        | dash    | flour |
|        | dash    | salt |
|        | dash    | pepper |
|        | dash    | sugar |
| 2      | cups    | milk |
|        |         | green beans |
| 1      | stick   | butter |

Spread the bottom of pan with sliced potatoes. Add a layer of onion slices, and cheese slices. Sprinkle with a dash of flour, salt, pepper, sugar, and 1/2 cup of milk. repeat again for the second layer. add butter, 1 1/2 cup of milk, cover with green beans. Bake until done.

*Mother Manning*

# Shalots onion dish

| Amount | Measure | Ingredient -- Preparation Method |
| --- | --- | --- |
| 2 1/2 | cups | shallots onions |
| 4 | tablespoons | oil |
| 3 | tablespoons | flour |
| 1/2 | tablespoon | sugar |
| 1/2 | tablespoon | salt |
| 3 | eggs | beaten |
| 1/2 | cup | milk |

Wash and cut up shallots. Top with oil. Saute onion in oil for 5 minutes. Make mixture of flour , sugar, salt, eggs, milk and beat well. Pour the mixture over the onions and stir. Cook for 3 to 4 minutes. Serve with bacon or sausage. Can also be served on a bed of rice.

# Sliced Liver

| Amount | Measure | Ingredient -- Preparation Method |
|--------|---------|----------------------------------|
|        |         | Sliced beef or pork liver        |
|        | dash    | salt and pepper                  |
|        |         | flour                            |
|        |         | oil                              |

Cut up beef or pork liver into strips. Season with salt and pepper. Coat with flour and fry in oil until done.

*Mother Manning*

# Smothered Chicken

| Amount | Measure | Ingredient -- Preparation Method |
|---|---|---|
| 1 | whole | chicken cut up |
| 2 | cups | water |
| 1 | can | chicken broth or cream of chicken soup |
| 1 | small | onion cut up |
| 1/2 | cup | celery and green pepper |
| 1/2 | stick | butter |
|  | dash | salt and pepper |
| 1 | tablespoon | flour |

Place chicken in pot with 2 cups of water, and 1 can of chicken broth or cream of chicken soup. Add onion, celery, green pepper, salt and pepper. Cook until chicken is tender. Make a paste with 1 tbs flour and water. Add to the chicken to make broth thick. Add butter and more water if needed. Cook an additional 15-20 minutes. Serve over rice or mashed potatoes.

# Sour Cream Chicken

| Amount | Measure | Ingredient -- Preparation Method |
|--------|---------|----------------------------------|
| 1 | whole | chicken cut up |
| 1 | 16 oz | sour cream |
|   |       | flour |

Preheat oven to 375. Season chicken to taste and coat with flour. Roll in sour cream and bake for 30 minutes or until done.

*Mother Manning*

# Special Boiled Corn

| Amount | Measure | Ingredient -- Preparation Method |
|--------|---------|----------------------------------|
|        |         | cleaned corn on the cob          |
|        |         | food coloring                    |
|        |         | butter                           |
|        |         | chili powder or salt             |

Boil corn about 25 minutes. When done let cool, then drop a few drops of food coloring on it. Rub corn with a small amount of chili powder.

# Special Hot Dogs

| Amount | Measure | Ingredient -- Preparation Method |
| --- | --- | --- |
| 1 | pack | hot dogs |
|   |   | white bread |
|   |   | butter |
|   |   | cheese is optional |

Spread butter on each side of the slices of white bread. Wrap each slice around the hot dog and bake for 13 minutes in a 325 degree oven. If you use cheese, place cheese on bread and the wrap around the hot dog and bake.

*Mother Manning*

# Steak & Mushroom

| Amount | Measure | Ingredient -- Preparation Method |
| --- | --- | --- |
| 1 | pound | steak |
|   | dash | salt, pepper and paprika |
| 1/2 | cup | flour |
| 1 | small | onion sliced |
| 1 | cup | mushroom |
| 1/2 | cup | apple juice or cooking wine |

Line bottom of pan with sliced onion and mushrooms. Season steak with salt, pepper and paprika.
Cover with flour. Place seasoned steak on top of onions and mushrooms. Pour apple juice or cooking wine over steak. Bake for 30-45 minutes in a 350 degree oven or until steak is tender.

# Stew Meat

| Amount | Measure | Ingredient -- Preparation Method |
|---|---|---|
| 2 | pounds | stew meat |
| 4 | cups | water |
| 1 | cup | cubed turnip bottoms |
| 2 | cups | cubed potatoes |
| 1/2 | cup | onion |
| 1/2 | cup | green pepper |
| 1/2 | cup | celery |
| 1 | can | tomatoes |
|  | dash | salt and pepper |

Place stew meat in pot with 4 cups of water and cook until almost done. Season with salt and pepper to taste. Next add 1 cup of cut up turnip bottoms, and 2 cups of cut up potatoes. Then add 1/2 cup each of onions, green pepper, and celery. Finally add one can of tomatoes and cook until done.

*Mother Manning*

# Stuffed Cabbage

| Amount | Measure | Ingredient -- Preparation Method |
|---|---|---|
| 1 | medium | cabbage |
| 1/2 | pound | ground beef |
| 1/2 | cup | rice (uncooked) |
| 1 | medium | onion cut up |
| 1/2 | cup | chopped green pepper |
| 1 | teaspoon | chili powder |
|  | dash | salt and pepper |
|  |  | tomato paste or sauce |
| 2 | cups | water |

Take the loose leaves from around the cabbage head. Cut the center part of the cabbage, and fill with the following mixture. (mixture): ground beef, uncooked rice, onion, green pepper, chili powder, salt, and pepper. Mix together with tomato paste or sauce. Put inside of cabbage, then take 3 of the loose cabbage leaves and put them over the top of the cabbage. Pin loose leaves down with tooth picks and then add water. Cook on top or in oven for 25-30 minutes or until cabbage is tender and ground beef is completely
done.

# Sunny Side Up Eggs

| Amount | Measure | Ingredient -- Preparation Method |
|--------|---------|----------------------------------|
|        |         | eggs                             |
|        |         | strips of cheese                 |

Slowly cook eggs, when almost done criss cross with strips of cheese.

*Mother Manning*

# Sweet and Sour Dish

| Amount | Measure | Ingredient -- Preparation Method |
| --- | --- | --- |
| 1 | pound | cubed chicken |
| 1 | can | sour kraut drained |
| 1 | small | sliced apple |
| 1 | small | onion |
| 1 | can | crushed pineapple |
| 3 1/2 | tablespoons | brown sugar |
| 2 | tablespoons | vinegar |
| 1 1/2 | cups | water |

Season chicken and place in deep pan or roaster. Mix remaining ingredients and add to chicken. Bake in a 350 degree oven for 30-45 minutes or until done.

# Sweet Pea Dumpling

| Amount | Measure | Ingredient -- Preparation Method |
|---|---|---|
| 2 | cups | sweet peas |
| 1/2 | cup | diced ham |
| 1 1/2 | cups | water |
| 1 | cup | milk |
| 1/2 | stick | butter |
| 1 | tablespoon | sugar |
|  |  | dumplings |
|  | dash | salt and pepper |

Combine sweet peas, ham, milk, water, and butter in a pot. Season with salt, pepper, and sugar. Cook for 25-30 minutes then drop dumplings into mixture and cook and additional 15-20 minutes. Add more water if needed.

*Mother Manning*

# Sweet Potatoe Balls

Amount    Measure        Ingredient -- Preparation Method
---------- -----------   ------------------------------------------
                         sweet potato mixture
                         flour
                         honey

Prepare sweet potato as for a pie. Add flour to the mixture. Form into balls, then glaze with honey. Bake in a 350 degree oven until done.

# Sweet Potatoe Souffle

| Amount | Measure | Ingredient -- Preparation Method |
|---|---|---|
| 3 | cups | cooked sweet potatoes |
| 3 |  | eggs slightly beaten |
| 2 | teaspoons | baking powder |
| 1/2 | cup | raisins |
| 1 1/2 | cups | whipping cream |
| 1 1/2 | cups | sugar |
| 1 | stick | butter melted |
| 1 | teaspoon | vanilla |
| 1/2 | teaspoon | nutmeg |
| 1/2 | cup | pet milk |

Mix 3 cups of mashed cooked sweet potatoes with 3 slightly beaten eggs, 2 tsp of baking powder, 1/2 cup of raisins, 1 1/2 cup of whipping cream, 1 1/2 cup of sugar, 1 stick butter melted, tsp of vanilla, 1/2 tsp of nutmeg and 1/2 cup of pet milk. Mix well and bake for 25-30 minutes in a 300 degree oven.

*Mother Manning*

# Traditional Beef Stew

| Amount | Measure | Ingredient -- Preparation Method |
|--------|---------|----------------------------------|
| 1 1/2  | pounds    | cubed stew meat |
| 2 1/2  | cups      | water |
| 1 1/2  | teaspoons | salt |
| 1/2    | teaspoon  | pepper |
| 1      | dash      | allspice |
| 1      | teaspoon  | tarragon |
| 2      | pounds    | potatoes |
| 1/2    | cup       | sliced carrots |
| 2      | pounds    | turnip bottoms |
| 1      | can       | tomatoes or 3 fresh tomatoes |
| 1/2    | cup       | celery |
| 1/2    | cup       | green pepper |

Coat stew meat with flour and brown in oil on all sides. Place browned meat in pot with water, salt, pepper, allspice and tarragon. Cook for 40 minutes. Add potatoes, sliced carrots, turnips bottoms, tomatoes, celery and green peppers. cook an additional 35 minutes adding water as needed.

# Turkey Legs

| Amount | Measure | Ingredient -- Preparation Method |
|--------|---------|----------------------------------|
|        |         | turkey legs                      |
| 1      | small   | onions                           |
| 1      | cup     | water                            |

Line your pan with sliced onions, then place the seasoned turkey legs on top of onions. Add 1 cup of water. Cook for 35-45 minutes in a 350 degree oven or until done.

# Veal Cutlets

| Amount | Measure | Ingredient -- Preparation Method |
|---|---|---|
| 2 | pounds | veal cutlet |
|  | dash | salt and pepper |
|  | flour |  |
| 1/2 | cup | onions, celery, green pepper |
| 1 | can | cream of chicken soup |
| 2 | cups | water |
| 2 | tablespoons | flour |
| 1/4 | cup | oil |

Season veal cutlets with salt and pepper, then coat with flour. Brown on both sides in a little oil and place aside. Saute onions, celery, green pepper in the oil then add cream of chicken soup and water. In a cup add 2 tbs of flour with a little of water to make a paste. Add this to the mixture. Add veal cutlets an simmer for 5-7 minutes. Serve on a bed of rice or noodles.

# *Desserts*

# Cherry Cake

| Amount | Measure | Ingredient -- Preparation Method |
|--------|---------|----------------------------------|
| 1 | box | cherry cake mix |
| 1 | tub | cool whip |
| 1 | jar | maraschino cherries |

Mix cake according to directions on box. Add chopped up maraschino cherries to mix and bake as directed. When cake is done frost with whip cream and serve with a cherry on top of each slice.

*Mother Manning*

# Coconut Cookies

| Amount | Measure | Ingredient -- Preparation Method |
|---|---|---|
| 2 | eggs | beaten |
| 1 | cup | sugar |
| 1 | cup | milk |
| 1 | stick | butter |
| 1 | teaspoon | vanilla extract |
| 1 1/2 | cups | flour |
| 2 | teaspoons | baking soda |
| 1 1/2 | cups | coconut |

Mix all ingredients together. Then drop from a spoon onto a greased cookie sheet. Bake about 10 minutes in a 275 degree oven or until done.

# Cookie Ideal

| Amount | Measure | Ingredient -- Preparation Method |
|--------|---------|----------------------------------|
| 1 | cookie | dough |
| 1 | small | orange |
| 1 | small | lemon |

Preheat oven to 350. Grate 1tbsp of the lemon and 1tbsp of the orange. Place cookies on ungreased cookie sheet and sprinkle with orange and lemon grated rind.

*Mother Manning*

# Corn Bread Cake

| Amount | Measure | Ingredient -- Preparation Method |
| --- | --- | --- |
| 1 1/2 | cups | corn meal |
| 1 | cup | flour |
| 3 | teaspoons | baking powder |
| 2 | | eggs |
| 1 | cup | sugar |
| 1 | cup | syrup |
| 1 | dash | soda |
| 2 1/2 | sticks | butter |
| 1 1/2 | cups | milk |
| 1 | teaspoon | vanilla flavoring |
| 1/2 | teaspoon | cinnamon |

Preheat oven to 350.
Combine all dry ingredient in a separate bowl
Cream butter and sugar together. Add eggs one at a time mixing after each addition.

Add syrup and vanilla to creamed ingredients. .
Alternate adding dry mixture to creamed mixture with milk. Mix well and bake at 350 for 30 minutes.

# Corn Bread Pudding

| Amount | Measure | Ingredient -- Preparation Method |
| --- | --- | --- |
| 2 1/2 | cups | already cooked corn bread |
| 1 | cup | sugar |
| 1 | egg | |
| 2 | cups | milk |
| 1 | teaspoon | vanilla flavoring |
| 1 | dash | nutmeg |
| 1 | tablespoon | flour |
| 1 | | Stick melted butter |

Preheat oven to 350. Crumble corn bread into pieces, spread on bottom of loaf pan.
Mix remaining ingredient and pour over corn bread. Bake for 20 minutes.

*Mother Manning*

# Dream Cake

| Amount | Measure | Ingredient -- Preparation Method |
| --- | --- | --- |
| 3 | sticks | butter |
| 2 1/2 | cups | sugar |
| 4 | | eggs |
| 3 | cups | flour sifted |
| 4 | teaspoons | baking powder |
| 1 1/2 | cups | pet milk |
| 1 1/2 | teaspoons | flavoring of your choice |
| 2 1/2 | cups | apple sauce |
| | | red food coloring |

Prehaet oven to 375. Cream 3 sticks of butter, with 2 1/2 cups of sugar, add 4 eggs and mix well. In a different bowl mix 3 cups of flour, 4 tsp baking powder, and sift into wet mixture. Add 1 1/2 cups of can milk, 1 1/2 tsp extracts of your choice and mix well. Add red food coloring to 2 1/2 cups of apple sauce until very pink, set aside. Pour 1/2 of cake mixture into greased cake pan, pour apple sauce over cake mixture and add remaining cake mixture. Bake for 30 minutes or until done. Frost with your favorite icing.

# Egg Custard Pie

| Amount | Measure | Ingredient -- Preparation Method |
|---|---|---|
| 6 | eggs | |
| 1 | can | pet milk |
| 1 | cup | sugar |
| 3 | tablespoons | corn starch |
| 4 | tablespoons | water |
| 3 | tablespoons | melted butter |
| 1 | teaspoon | lemon or vanillla flavoring |
| 1 | 9 in | uncooked pie crust |

Preheat oven to 350. Mix all ingredients together and bake in uncooked pie crust for about 40 minutes.
Brown lightly under broiler.

*Mother Manning*

# Egg Pudding

| Amount | Measure | Ingredient -- Preparation Method |
| --- | --- | --- |
| 5 | | eggs |
| 1 | cup | sugar |
| 3 | tablespoons | cornstarch |
| 2 | cups | pet milk |
| 3 | tablespoons | melted butter |
| 1 | teaspoon | vanilla flavoring |
| 1/2 | teaspoon | nutmeg |
| 1 1/2 | cups | flour |
| 1 1/2 | teaspoons | baking powder |
| 1 | teaspoon | salt |
| 1/2 | stick | butter melted |
| | dash | water |

Preheat oven to 350. Add sugar, cornstarch, pet milk, vanilla, nutmeg and 3 tbs of melted butter to beaten eggs. Pour into baking dish. In a separate bowl add flour, baking powder, salt, 1/2 stick of melted butter with enough water to make paste. Spoon paste over the egg mixture and bake until brown. Bake for 25 minutes or until done.

# Fruit Cake

| Amount | Measure | Ingredient -- Preparation Method |
|--------|---------|----------------------------------|
| 1 2/3  | cups    | sugar |
| 1      | cup     | brown sugar and glazed fruit |
| 3      | sticks  | butter |
| 3      | teaspoons | baking powder |
| 3      |         | eggs |
| 2 2/3  | cups    | flour |
| 2      | cups    | milk |
| 1      | teaspoon | flavoring of your choice |
| 1/2    | teaspoon | clove |
| 1/2    | teaspoon | nutmeg & cinnamon |
| 1/2    | cup each of | raisins, dates, black walnuts, pecans |

Mix together sugar, brown sugar and eggs until creamy. Add milk and flavoring and mix well. In separate bowl mix 2 1/2 cups of flour, baking powder and spices then add to wet mixture and mix well. In another bowl add glazed fruit, raisins, dates, black walnuts and pecans. Mix in 3 tbsp of sugar and flour. Finally combine this with other mixture, and mix well. Pour into a greased cake pan and bake about 60 minutes in a 350 degree oven.

*Mother Manning*

# Green Tomato Pie

| Amount | Measure | Ingredient -- Preparation Method |
|---|---|---|
| 4 |  | green tomatoes |
| 2 1/2 | cups | water |
| 1 1/2 | cups | sugar |
| 1 | stick | butter |
| 1 | teaspoon | vanilla flavoring |
| 1/2 | teaspoon | nutmeg |
|  |  | flouring dumplings |

Cut up green tomatoes and place in pot. Cover tomatoes with 2 1/2 cups of water. Next add 1 1/2 cups or sugar, 1 stick of butter, 1 tsp of vanilla, and 1/2 tsp of nutmeg. Cook mixture for 15-20 minutes. Add a few small dumplings into the pot, and then place mixture in a baking dish. Cover baking dish with one crust, then make 2-3 slits in crust. Finally bake about 15-20 minutes and enjoy.

# Hot Cocoa

| Amount | Measure | Ingredient -- Preparation Method |
|---|---|---|
| 3 | cups | milk |
| 3 | tablespoons | cocoa mix |
| 4 | tablespoons | hot water |
| 4 | tablespoons | sugar |
| 1/2 | tablespoon | vanilla |
|  | dash | nutmeg |

Mix cocoa mix with hot water and milk. Add sugar, vanilla and dash of nutmeg. Heat until very hot and enjoy.

*Mother Manning*

# Ice Cream Cups

| Amount | Measure | Ingredient -- Preparation Method |
|---|---|---|
| | | ice cream mix |
| | small | cups |
| | | crushed peppermint candy |

Make ice cream following instructions on ice cream mix. Place in cups, top with crushed peppermint candy then place in freezer until set.

# Loaf Cake

| Amount | Measure | Ingredient -- Preparation Method |
|--------|---------|----------------------------------|
|        |         | done loaf cake                   |
|        |         | Cool Whip®                       |
|        |         | sweeten strawberries             |

Cover loaf cake with cool whip and strawberries.

# Oatmeal Cake

| Amount | Measure | Ingredient -- Preparation Method |
| --- | --- | --- |
| 2 1/3 | cups | sugar |
| 3 | sticks | butter |
| 3 | | eggs |
| 1 1/2 | cups | flour |
| 1 1/2 | cups | oatmeal |
| 3 | teaspoons | baking powder |
| 1 | teaspoon | flavoring of your choice |
| 1/2 | teaspoon | mace |
| 1 1/2 | cups | pet milk |

Preheat oven to 375. Grease two 8x10 cake pans. Cream sugar and butter, add eggs one at a time mixing well after each. In another bowl mix dry ingredients and add to wet mixture alternating with pet milk. Add flavoring. Bake for 30-35 minutes. Frost with butter cream frosting.

# Peach and Cabbage Cobbler

| Amount | Measure | Ingredient -- Preparation Method |
|---|---|---|
| 3 | cups | peaches |
| 1 | cup | white part of the cabbage |
| 1 1/2 | cups | sugar |
| 2 | cups | peach juice or water |
| 1 | teaspoon | vanilla |
| 1/2 | teaspoon | nutmeg |
| 1 | stick | butter |
|  |  | dumplings |
|  |  | pie crust |

Cook sliced peaches, with cut up white part of the cabbage, sugar and peach juice. Add vanilla, nutmeg and butter. Then drop a few flour dumplings in. Place in a baking dish, cover with pie crust. Cut 3 slits in top and bake for 20-30 minutes in a 300 degree oven until done.

*Mother Manning*

# Peach Cobbler

| Amount | Measure | Ingredient -- Preparation Method |
|---|---|---|
| 4 | cups | fresh peaches |
| 1 1/2 | cups | sugar |
| 1 | stick | butter |
| 1/2 | teaspoon | nutmeg |
| 1/2 | teaspoon | vanilla flavoring |
| | | Dumplings |
| 1 1/2 | cups | flour |
| | dash | salt |
| 2 | teaspoons | baking powder |
| 4 | tablespoons | oil |
| | | milk |
| | | butter |

Cook peaches with sugar, butter, nutmeg, and vanilla until done. Place peach mixture into baking dish. For dumpling mixture combine the dry ingredients first and then add oil and enough milk to make batter soft. Spread over the peaches a spoon full at a time. Dot with butter and bake for 20 minutes in a 375 degree oven or until done.

# Peach Delight

| Amount | Measure | Ingredient -- Preparation Method |
| --- | --- | --- |
| 5 1/2 | cups | bread crumbs |
| 2 1/2 | sticks | butter melted |
| 1 1/3 | cups | sugar |
| 3 | dashes | nutmeg |
| 3 | cups | peaches sliced |
| 1 | teaspoon | vanilla flavoring |
| 4 | tablespoons | flour |

First mix 3 cups of bread crumbs with 1 stick of butter melted, 3 tbs of sugar and a dash of nutmeg. Mix together and spread on bottom of pan or dish. Next mix 3 cups of sliced peaches, 1 cup of sugar, 4 tbs of flour, 1 stick melted butter, 1 tsp of vanilla and a dash of nutmeg. Spread this mixture on top of bread crumbs. Finally mix together 2 1/2 cups of bread crumbs, 1/2 stick of butter melted, 3 tbs sugar, and a dash of nutmeg. Spread this mixture over top of the peaches. Bake for 25-30 minutes in a 350 degree oven. Enjoy.

*Mother Manning*

## Peach in a Blanket

| Amount | Measure | Ingredient -- Preparation Method |
| --- | --- | --- |
| 1 | can | peach halves |
|  |  | prepared dough |
|  |  | nutmeg |
|  |  | butter |
| 1/2 | cup | sugar |
|  |  | juice from peaches |
| 3 | tablespoons | butter |
| 1 | teaspoon | vanilla flavoring |
|  | dash | nutmeg |
| 1 | can | biscuits can be used for dough |

Make a batch of dough. Pinch off a piece about the size of a egg. Roll it out and fill with a peach half, a dash of nutmeg, butter and sugar. Fold together and place in pan. Make as many as you can then cover with juice mixture. Mix peach juice with sugar, butter, vanilla and nutmeg. Pour over peaches and bake until done in a 275 degree oven.

# Peach Parfait

| Amount | Measure | Ingredient -- Preparation Method |
| --- | --- | --- |
| 2 1/2 | cups | cooked peaches |
| 1 | can | pet milk |
| 3 | eggs | beaten slightly |
| 1 | stick | butter melted |
| 2 1/2 | tablespoons | cornstarch or flour |
| 1 | teaspoon | vanilla extract |
|  | dash | nutmeg |
| 1 | cup | sugar |

Mix all ingredients well. Bake for 20-25 minutes in a 350 degree oven or until done.

# Peach Pie

| Amount | Measure | Ingredient -- Preparation Method |
| --- | --- | --- |
| 3 | cups | peaches sliced |
| 1 1/2 | cups | sugar |
| 1 | stick | butter |
| 2 | tablespoons | flour |
|  | dash | nutmeg |
| 1 | teaspoon | vanilla extract |
|  |  | pan cake mix |

Place sliced peaches on bottom of pan. Then season with sugar, butter, flour, nutmeg, and vanilla extract. Make batter as pan cake mix. Spread pan cake batter on top of peaches and dot with butter. Bake until done in a 275 degree oven.

# Peach Pudding

| Amount | Measure | Ingredient -- Preparation Method |
| --- | --- | --- |
| 2 | cups | cooked peaches |
| 2 | cups | bread crumbs |
| 2 1/2 | cups | milk |
| 2 | | eggs beaten |
| 1 1/2 | cups | sugar |
| 1 | stick | butter |
| | dash | nutmeg |
| | dash | cinnamon |
| 1 | Teaspoon | vanilla extract |

Preheat oven to 350. Mix all ingredients well, pourn into cake pan and bake for 25-30 minutes.

*Mother Manning*

# Poor Man's Pudding

| Amount | Measure | Ingredient -- Preparation Method |
| --- | --- | --- |
| 1 | cup | flour |
| 1 | cup | corn meal |
| 1 1/2 | cups | bread crumbs |
| 2 | cups | sugar |
| 2 | cups | milk |
| 3 | | eggs |
| 3 | sticks | butter |
| 3 | teaspoons | baking powder |
| 1/2 | teaspoon | nutmeg |
| 1 | teaspoon | vanilla |

Preheat oven to 375 degree. Mix all ingredients, beat well then bake in loaf pan for 35-40 minutes.

# Pound Cake

| Amount | Measure | Ingredient -- Preparation Method |
| --- | --- | --- |
| 3 | cups | flour |
| 4 | teaspoons | baking powder |
| 4 | | eggs |
| 2 1/2 | cups | sugar |
| 3 | sticks | butter |
| 1 | can | pet milk |
| 2 | teaspoons | vanilla flavoring |

Cream sugar and butter together, add eggs one at a time mixing well after each addition. Then add flavoring. Mix baking powder, add flour 1 cup at a time alternating with milk to wet mixture. Beat well with mixer. Bake in greased and floured cake pan. Bake for 50-60 minutes in a 350 degree oven, or until tooth pick comes out completely dry.

*Mother Manning*

# Rainbow Cake

| Amount | Measure | Ingredient -- Preparation Method |
| --- | --- | --- |
| 2 1/2 | cups | sugar |
| 3 | sticks | butter |
| 3 |  | eggs |
| 3 | cups | flour |
| 2 | cups | pet milk |
| 1 1/2 | teaspoons | vanilla flavoring |
| 3 | drops | red/ green/ blue food coloring |

Mix sugar and butter until creamy, then add eggs and beat more. Next add flour, pet milk, and vanilla then mix well. Place batter into a loaf pan and add drops of red/ green/ blue food coloring. Take a knife and swirl coloring through the batter a few times. Bake in a greased pan for about 25-30 minutes in a 375 degree oven. Frost with your favorite frosting.

# Rainbow Pop Corn

| Amount | Measure | Ingredient -- Preparation Method |
|--------|---------|----------------------------------|
| 1      | bag     | popcorn                          |
|        |         | colored marshmallow              |
|        |         | food coloring                    |

Pop your popcorn as usual. When finished popping and still hot add a few small colored marshmallows and a few drops of food coloring (red, blue, yellow). Stir well and enjoy.

*Mother Manning*

# Raisin Chiffon Pie

| Amount | Measure | Ingredient -- Preparation Method |
| --- | --- | --- |
| 2 | cups | raisins |
| 1 1/2 | cups | brown sugar |
| 1/2 | cup | chopped nuts |
| 2 | tablespoons | cornstarch |
| 1/2 | cup | pet milk |
| 1 | cup | water |
| 1/2 | cup | orange juice |
| 1 | teaspoon | vanilla extract |

Mix all ingredients together in a sauce pan, and cook for about 5-10 minutes. Pour cooked ingredients into a ready pie crust and then cover with an additional crust making a double crust. Finally bake for 30-35 minutes in a 350 degree oven.

# Raisin Delight Cake

| Amount | Measure | Ingredient -- Preparation Method |
|---|---|---|
| 2 1/2 | cups | sugar |
| 1 1/2 | cups | flour |
| 1 1/2 | cups | corn meal |
| 3 | | eggs |
| 2 | teaspoons | baking powder or dash of baking soda |
| 1 | cup | milk |
| 3 | sticks | butter |
| 1 | teaspoon | vanilla flavoring |
| 1/2 | teaspoon | cinnamon |
| 1 | Cup | raisin |
| 1 | cup | pecan |
| 1 | cup | dates |
| 1/2 | cup | flour |

Mix sugar, flour, cornmeal, eggs, soda, baking powder, milk, vanilla, butter, and cinnamon. In separate bowl combine raisins, pecan, dates and flour. Add to other mixture, mix well and bake 40 minutes in a 300 degree oven or until done.

*Mother Manning*

# Raisin Delight

| Amount | Measure | Ingredient -- Preparation Method |
|---|---|---|
| 1/2 | cup | chopped nuts |
| 1 | cup | raisins |
| 1 3/4 | cups | flour |
| 2 | teaspoons | baking powder |
| 1 | teaspoon | ginger, cinnamon, vanilla |
| 2 |  | eggs |
| 1 | stick | butter melted |
| 1 | cup | pet milk |

Mix chopped nuts, raisin and 4 tbsp of flour together and set aside. In another mixing bowl mix remaining flour, baking powder, ginger, cinnamon, vanilla, eggs, butter, and evaporated milk (may need more then 1 cup of milk). add nuts and raisin, then mix well. Bake for 25-30 minutes in a 350 degree oven.

# Raspberry Pie

| Amount | Measure | Ingredient -- Preparation Method |
|--------|---------|----------------------------------|
| 1 | box | raspberry pudding mix |
| 2 | cups | crushed or cut up raspberries |
| 1 |  | graham cracker crust |
|   |  | cool whip |

Make pudding according to instructions, (can be instant or cooked pudding) add raspberries and mix well. Put mixture into graham cracker crust and top with cool whip. Chill and then serve. Enjoy!

*Mother Manning*

# Rice Parfait

| Amount | Measure | Ingredient -- Preparation Method |
|---|---|---|
| 2 | cups | pet milk |
| 3 | eggs | beaten |
| 1 | cup | sugar |
| 2 | tablespoons | cornstarch or flour |
| 1 | teaspoon | vanilla flavoring |
| 1 | stick | butter |
| 1 1/2 | cups | cooked rice |
|  |  | dash nutmeg |

Mix all ingredients together and bake in a baking dish for 25 minutes or until done. Bake in a 350 degree oven.

# Rice Pudding

| Amount | Measure | Ingredient -- Preparation Method |
| --- | --- | --- |
| 2 1/2 | cups | cooked rice |
| 1 | cup | crushed pineapple |
| 1/2 | cup | raisin |
| 2 | tablespoons | flour |
| 1 | cup | sugar |
| 1 1/2 | sticks | butter |
| 2 | cups | pet milk or regular milk |
| 2 | | eggs |
| 1 | teaspoon | vanilla flavoring |
| | dash | cinnamon and nutmeg |

Mix all ingredients and bake in a 350 degree oven until done.

# About the Author

Mother Manning, as she is called by her family and friends, has been awakened by the Holy Spirit since the tender young age of 63, with the inspiration to write recipes and poems. She would keep a pen and paper next to her bed and when directed by the Holy Spirit, would write until the Holy Spirit would stop giving them to her. She has amassed a collection of over 200 recipes and poems.

The Holy Spirit appeared to her a long time ago and said, you are one of God's chosen people. She was to pray for the sick and needy also to praise his name. She has done this for years and has been blessed by the Holy Spirit to be able to bring her recipes to the public to be shared by all.

May God Bless All.

Printed in the United States
92851LV00007B/129/A